Superflex takes on Brain Eater and the Team of UnthinkaBots™

2nd Edition

WRITTEN BY:
Stephanie Madrigal
Michelle Garcia Winner
Pamela Crooke

Superflex® takes on Brain Eater and the Team of UnthinkaBots™, 2nd Edition

Stephanie Madrigal, Michelle Garcia Winner, and Pamela Crooke

Copyright © 2023 Think Social Publishing, Inc.

All Rights Reserved except as noted herein.

NOTE: The Social Thinking Methodology is made up of language-based curricula, frameworks, and strategies. Because our methodology is dynamic, the language we use to teach evolves along with the culture at large combined with the feedback we get directly from our clients and community. This volume replaces the term Unthinkable with UnthinkaBot and includes minimal but important updates to descriptive language and character artwork to teach basic concepts.

Outside of the specific use described below, all other reproduction/copying, adaptation, conversion to electronic format, or sharing/distribution of content, through print or electronic means, is not permitted without written permission from Think Social Publishing, Inc. (TSP).

This includes prohibition of any use of any content or materials from this product as part of an adaptation or derivative work you create for posting on a personal or business website, TeachersPayTeachers, YouTube, Pinterest, Facebook, or any other social media or information sharing site in existence now or in the future, whether free or for a fee. Exceptions are made, upon written request, for product reviews, articles, and blogposts.

TSP grants permission to the owner of this book to use and/or adapt content in print or electronic form, only for direct in-classroom/school/home or in-clinic use with your own students/clients/children, and with the primary stakeholders in that individual's life, which includes parents/caregivers and direct service personnel. The copyright for any adaptation of content owned by TSP remains with TSP as a derivative work.

Social Thinking, Superflex, The Unthinkables, The UnthinkaBots, The Thinkables, and We Thinkers! GPS are trademarks belonging to TSP.

Translation of this product can only be done in accordance with our TRANSLATION POLICY found on our intellectual property website page here: https://www.socialthinking.com/intellectual-property.

And, visit our intellectual property page to find detailed TERMS OF USE information and a DECISION-TREE that cover copyright, trademark, and intellectual property topics and questions governing the use of our materials.

ISBN: 978-1-962301-02-2

Think Social Publishing, Inc.
404 Saratoga Avenue, Suite 200
Santa Clara, CA 95050
Tel: (408) 557-8595
Fax: (408) 557-8594

Illustrated by Kyle Richardson

This book was printed and bound in the United States by Mighty Color Printing.
TSP is a sole source provider of Social Thinking products in the U.S.
Books may be purchased online at www.socialthinking.com

This illustrated storybook is dedicated to all the professionals, caregivers, and students who have helped develop Superflex, the Unthinkables/UnthinkaBots, and the Superflex Academy.

All children can benefit from the teaching that is at the foundation of the Social Thinking Methodology. The Superflex series, including this storybook, is for both neurotypical and Neurodivergent students who have solid language and academic learning. The book can be used in the classroom, small group settings, 1:1 teaching, or at home.

Recommended Teaching & Learning Pathway for using the Superflex Series

3-Step Pathway for kids ages 5-10*

1

Use the *You Are a Social Detective!* 2nd Ed. storybook and Teaching Curriculum first to introduce key Social Thinking concepts/Vocabulary to build social awareness.

2

After building social awareness and a social vocabulary, depending on the age of your student, introduce Superflex to teach about self-regulation toward behavior change.

3

Use any other Superflex books, games, and visuals AFTER teaching the Superflex Curriculum to take learning to a deeper level.

If you're working with kids ages 9-12

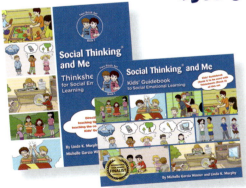

Start with Social Detective.

Next, *Social Thinking and Me* is used BEFORE or alongside teaching the Superflex Curriculum.

This two-book set helps deepen students' understanding of core Social Thinking concepts and gives them lots of practice to build stronger social competencies.

For kids aging out of Superflex (age 10+)

Start with *Social Thinking and Me* (if not already taught).

Next, move on to *Social Fortune or Social Fate.* (ages 10+)

* Some younger kids with social learning differences may need more time building their Social Detective skills. Wait to start Superflex with them until around age 8.

Find articles about teaching Superflex plus other books and teaching materials at www.SocialThinking.com

One Step at a Time!

Cautions and Information About the Use of This Material

Superflex Takes on Brain Eater and the Team of UnthinkBots is a storybook in our Superflex series designed to help children learn more about their own social behavior and strategies to regulate it. As charming and captivating as Superflex and the Team of UnthinkaBots are to students, this is *not* a starting place for teaching. Social Thinking Vocabulary and related concepts need to be first introduced to help children explore what it means to think social, to learn to be social observers and problem solvers, and understand the relationship between social thoughts and social behavioral expectations.

To be used effectively, caregivers and educators need to start at the beginning, introduce core concepts, and work through the Superflex Curriculum *before* sharing this storybook (or others to follow) with children. Books should be introduced in this order (see note if working with older kids):

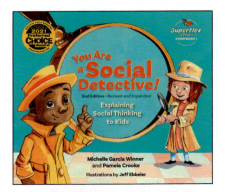

1. *You Are a Social Detective!*, 2nd Edition storybook and the companion *You Are a Social Detective!, 2nd Ed. Teaching Curriculum and Support Guide*

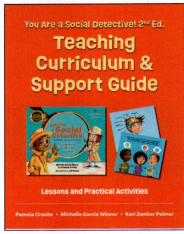

2. *Superflex Curriculum and Teaching Guide* that also includes the storybook *Superflexes Take on Rock Brain and the StuckBots*

Once these books have been introduced, adults are free to move on to any of the Superflex series books, games, music, or visual supports we have produced to date, in any order that meets the child's social learning needs or interests.

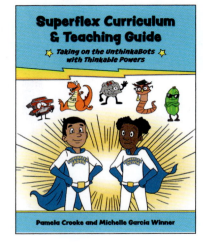

In *You Are a Social Detective,* children are introduced--through child-friendly illustrations and language--to core concepts that make up the Social Thinking® Methodology. Use the companion *You Are a Social Detective! 2nd Ed. Teaching Curriculum & Support Guide*, an easy-to-use curriculum that fits into your current teaching day. The storybook introduces students to core social emotional learning (SEL) concepts, and the curriculum provides

10 fun, structured lesson plans and visual tools to support building students' social attention, social interpretation, and self-awareness—the foundation for social emotional learning for everyone.

The *Superflex Curriculum and Teaching Guide* includes 25 evidence-informed, interactive quests that help students develop increased self-awareness around which situations and activities pose potential social hurdles, and then equip learners with proactive strategies for problem solving through the lens of using their own unique superpowers.

Children are introduced to the Superflex Academy and learn about a set of UnthinkaBots, who represent areas of struggle for all of us (adults and children alike), and Thinkable characters, who represent the flexible thinking and super strengths that allow us all to manage these daily challenges. By activating "Thinkable" strategies, students transform into their own "Superflex" superhero character who allows them to self-regulate in various situations and meet their own personal and social goals.

Adults can learn more about the Social Thinking Methodology in the book *Why Teach Social Thinking?* (Winner, 2013). Many free articles, webinars, and information about additional resources can be found at www.socialthinking.com.

Note: If you're teaching Superflex in a general education classroom, or starting Superflex with kids a little older, we suggest adding another book into the teaching series: *Social Thinking and Me*. This two-book set, aimed at kids ages 9-12, takes a deeper look into core Social Thinking concepts and helps kids get the practice they need to integrate this new information into everyday activities. See the Learning Pathways page for when to introduce it into the teaching series.

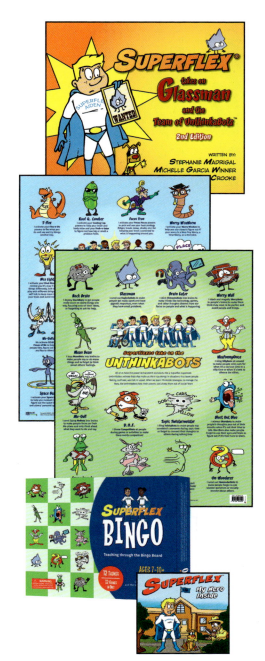

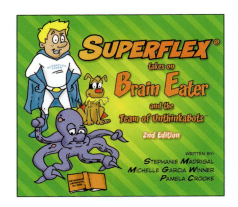

About This Book

In *Superflex Takes on Brain Eater and the Team of UnthinkaBots*, 2nd Edition, children become familiar with some social learning strategies they can use to help them manage Brain Eater and the DistractoBots' powers to distract their brains from focusing on what is expected. Although the story introduces specific strategies, not all strategies presented in the book will apply to every child. Caregivers and educators should closely evaluate what strategies are a match for each child and encourage them to identify what strategies they do and don't like.

The authors recognize that many other strategies can be used to help students better focus their attention. Social Thinking is not a stand-alone teaching curriculum and integrates well with other methods. The authors encourage adults to brainstorm ideas with other team members as well as explore other resources and the Internet for additional tools and ideas.

Using the Series: Things to Keep in Mind

- Children who will benefit from the Superflex curriculum are those who can differentiate well between fantasy and reality. They are encouraged to think about and understand that Superflex is a pretend character, and should be able to imagine they can transform themselves into their own superflexible superhero and use their own strategies for problem solving. This is a very different concept than pretending to be a superhero in a play situation. Pre-teach children that managing an UnthinkaBot is something that happens in their brains and is not a battle with their bodies. Children who struggle with these ideas may not be good candidates for and of the books in the Superflex series.

- The concepts in this book are best suited for students ages 8-11 with social learning differences. While many neurotypical students ages 5-7 will also find this material engaging and helpful, students of that age with social learning differences may find it too demanding too soon in their social learning lives!

- If students protest or don't enjoy this idea of superheroes, then please discontinue using this curriculum as a teaching tool and spend more time helping those children learn about the social world that surrounds them. Not every child is ready to take on their own personal program for self-regulation.

- The ultimate goal is to help children become better observers of social information and improve their responses and related social skills.

Congratulations! If you are reading this story, you've probably been picked to be a student at the Superflex Academy. At the Academy, you will learn how to become your own Superflex, a special kind of superhero.

You will study the sneaky ways of the Team of UnthinkaBots, who would like to get into the thinking inside your brain and get you to do or say things that show you aren't thinking about others. In this book you will learn from a Thinkable character, Focus Tron, who will give Aiden and others some ideas about how to manage Brain Eater and the DistractoBots.

Part of your Superflex training is to get to know each and every one of these UnthinkaBots--in case you need to work on managing them! Reading this story is one of the many fun things you will get to do while attending the very important Superflex Academy.

Along this adventure there will also be fun Social Town facts and quizzes to show your Superflex smarts. Possible answers can be found on the last pages of the book.

The UnthinkaBots

Worry Wall
I stack and magnify WorryBots in people's brains to make them think they need to be perfect and avoid people and things.

Blurt Out Blue
I release BlurtBots to make people's thoughts pop out of their mouths when it's not their time to talk. BlurtBots also make people forget to use their eyes and brain to figure out if it's their turn to share.

D.O.F.
I throw CompetiBots at people during games or activities to make them overly competitive!

Brain Eater
I stick DistractoBots into brains to make things like technology, games, and other thoughts distract from our focus on people and what is happening.

WasFunnyOnce
I sling SillyBots all around to make people miss cues for when it's a serious time or a silly time or when it's best to silence the sillies.

Energy Hare-y
I spring EnergyBots into people's bodies to make them use more or less energy than needed for what is happening and forget to use their energy managing strategies.

Body Drifter
I send DriftBots to push or pull bodies away from others or make them wander away from where they are supposed to be.

Glassman
I send out ExplodaBots to make people get really upset and have gigantic responses, even when they have small problems.

Un-Wonderer
I send out UnwonderBots to make people forget to ask wonder questions or socially wonder about others.

Space Invader
I send CloseBot flares to make people pop into other people's space bubble or touch others' stuff by crossing their stuff bubble.

Mean Bean
I toss MeanBots into brains to make people say or do mean things and to forget to think about others' feelings.

Rock Brain
I deploy StuckBots to get people really stuck on doing things one way, focusing only on their ideas, or forgetting to ask for help.

Me-Gull
I send flying MeBots into brains to make people focus on their Me-plans and only think about what they want to do and say.

Topic Twistermeister
I fling TwistaBots to make people say unrelated comments during *topic time* or forget to connect their thoughts to others during *talking time*.

The Team of UnthinkaBots has been around a long time, invading the brains of Social Town citizens! In Social Town, people live together and think about each other every day.

In this story, Brain Eater and others will try their luck at taking over Social Town. All of the UnthinkaBots are pretty clever, and they find ways to combine their powers.

You will see UnthinkaBots lurking in the corners of some pages, just waiting to help Brain Eater. When you see them, try to imagine what you might do if that UnthinkaBot was in your brain.

You see, each of us can become our own Superflex superhero that looks just like us. When the UnthinkaBots are active, the Superflex Brain Shifter sends out a message for all Superflexes, everywhere, to transform themselves into their Superflexes.

SUPERFLEXES remember to...

- be flexible thinkers
- use their flexible thinking strategies to manage the UnthinkaBots
- be thinking of many different ways to solve problems
- help other Superflexes when UnthinkaBots are near

THE UNTHINKABOT: BRAIN EATER

- Makes it hard for someone to focus on what they are supposed to be doing or to focus on others while in a group.

- Is good at finding things that a person enjoys thinking about, like video games, and filling that person's brain with those thoughts so it's hard to pay attention to anything else.

- Gets citizens distracted by things they see around them, like pictures or posters in a room. When that happens, citizens can miss out on what others expect them to focus on. Other people may feel like citzens are not listening, participating, and even that the citizens don't like the other people they are with.

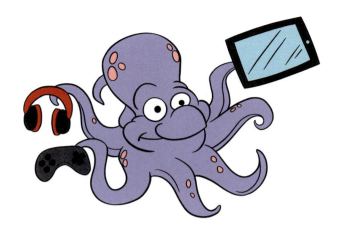

Brain Eater is one of the most common UnthinkaBots. Remember: most of us (adults too!) have Brain Eater's DistractoBots in our brains at times. Brain Eater sticks DistractoBots into people's brains to pull them away from what they are learning or doing.

Each person's DistractoBots look just like the thing that distracts them the most. Some are shaped like a video game controller while another person's bots might look like a book or toy or pet.

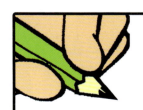

Activity Alert!

Draw a picture of what your DistractoBots might look like.

Hint: You can have many different types of DistractoBots.

Aiden hurries to get himself ready for school. He is supposed to meet his friend Matt.

Aiden goes to his friend Matt's house so they can walk to school together.

When they get to Matt's room, they find him still in his pajamas and playing on his computer. "Matt, why aren't you ready to go?" his mom asks.

Superflex Academy Lesson:
FOCUSING ON DAILY TO DOs

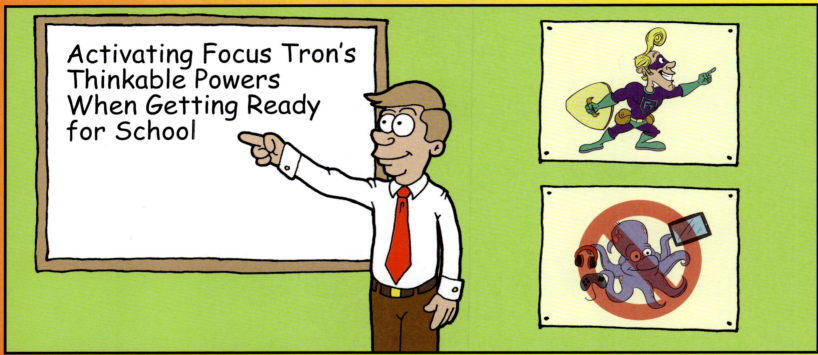

Today we are going to learn about how to activate a few Thinkable powers to manage Brain Eater and the DistractoBots. Let's start by thinking about our Daily TO DOs. Brain Eater loves to get into our brains to stop us from getting through our TO DO lists.

We all have lots and lots of TO DO lists during the day. Sometimes people call TO DOs chores or jobs or even routines. Adults have TO DOs too!

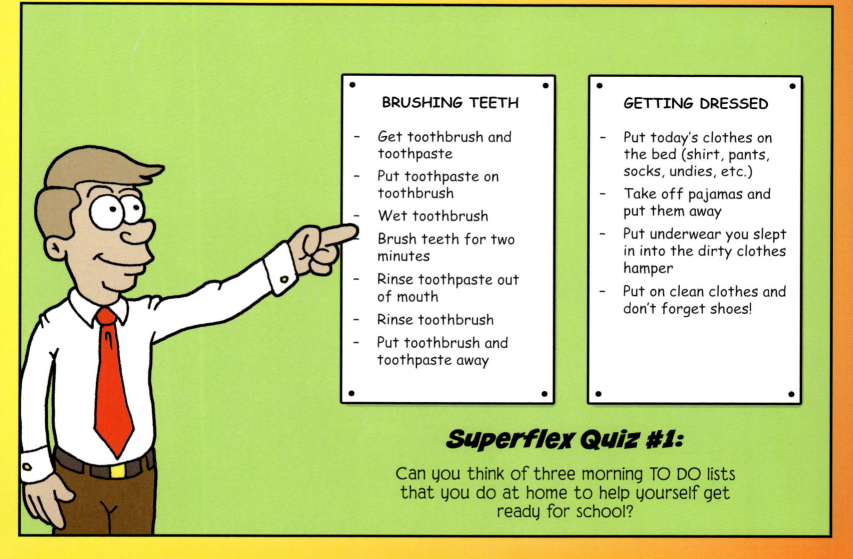

BRUSHING TEETH

- Get toothbrush and toothpaste
- Put toothpaste on toothbrush
- Wet toothbrush
- Brush teeth for two minutes
- Rinse toothpaste out of mouth
- Rinse toothbrush
- Put toothbrush and toothpaste away

GETTING DRESSED

- Put today's clothes on the bed (shirt, pants, socks, undies, etc.)
- Take off pajamas and put them away
- Put underwear you slept in into the dirty clothes hamper
- Put on clean clothes and don't forget shoes!

Superflex Quiz #1:

Can you think of three morning TO DO lists that you do at home to help yourself get ready for school?

Focus Tron Tip: If you use a checklist, you can focus on one chore at a time so you can finish it and move on to the next chore. Sometimes we add a 'break time' to the checklist to give our brain a rest before going on to the next chore. Usually, but not always, the chores on a checklist are written in the order they should be completed.

CHECKLIST:

- Get dressed
- Put pajamas away
- Brush hair
- Brush teeth
- Eat breakfast
- Pack lunch to take to school

Sometimes, if you work hard and stay focused on finishing all your chores, you may even have extra time to do something fun before you leave for school.

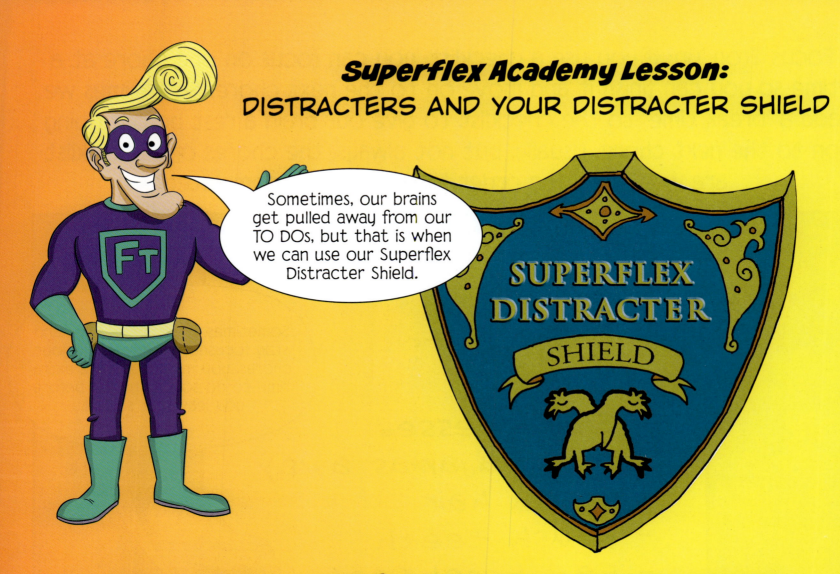

Superflex Academy Lesson:
DISTRACTERS AND YOUR DISTRACTER SHIELD

Sometimes, our brains get pulled away from our TO DOs, but that is when we can use our Superflex Distracter Shield.

Distracters are powerful because they pull your brain away from concentrating on your chores or things you need to do in school. Luckily, we can activate Focus Tron's powerful Distracter Shield! But first, we need to learn a little bit more about what might be distracters.

Distracters are things like video games, a book you enjoy reading, building sets, train schedules, etc. Brain Eater is the master of trying to get you to focus on your distracters! The Superflex Distracter Shield reminds you that you have the power to shield your brain from your distracting thoughts.

But Brain Eater sends DistractoBots into our brains. It takes practice to use your Superflex Distracter Shield. Every time you get just a little bit better at using it, we call that improvement!

Superflex Quiz #2:

Where would you put your Superflex Distracter Shield at home? At school?

Superflex Quiz #3:

How do you feel when you quickly finish your TO DOs at home? At school?

Matt realized that Brain Eater was trying to invade his brain by getting him distracted with the computer.

What do you think Matt's DistractoBots looked like in his brain?

Phew! Matt put his Superflex Distracter Shield over his computer and looked at his checklist to see what he had left to do.

He raced to get his clothes and go to the bathroom to finish getting ready.

Mom and Aiden were happy to see that Matt was able to focus his attention and manage Brain Eater from gaining more power.

Superflex Quiz #4:

How did you do today getting your chores done at home?

Matt got ready and the boys were off to school. Aiden was happy because he knew that if they were late again, his mom said he would have to stop walking to school with Matt.

Superflex Academy Lesson:
LEARNING TO AVOID AND MANAGE DISTRACTIONS IN THE CLASSROOM

Superflex Quiz #5:

Can you think of one Inside the Brain Distracter (ITBD) and one Outside the Brain Distracter (OTBD) that take your brain off track?

Superflex Academy Lesson:
KEEPING YOUR BRAIN IN THE GROUP

FOCUS FACT
When our bodies leave the group, our brains and focus usually do too.

Now that Haley's body is away from the group, she might miss part of the lesson. Other kids might get distracted and confused, wondering what she's doing.

So when we're in a group, even a whole class, we have to try to keep the group together by keeping our brains and bodies in the group and not letting them roll away.

If we can do this, we'll keep Brain Eater's DistractoBots and Body Drifter's DriftBots out of our brains!!

Superflex Quiz #6:

Give an example of your brain rolling away from the group and your body rolling away from the group.

Suddenly, Aiden was excused from class when he noticed the Superflex Brain Shifter was shaking. It trasmitted the following message:

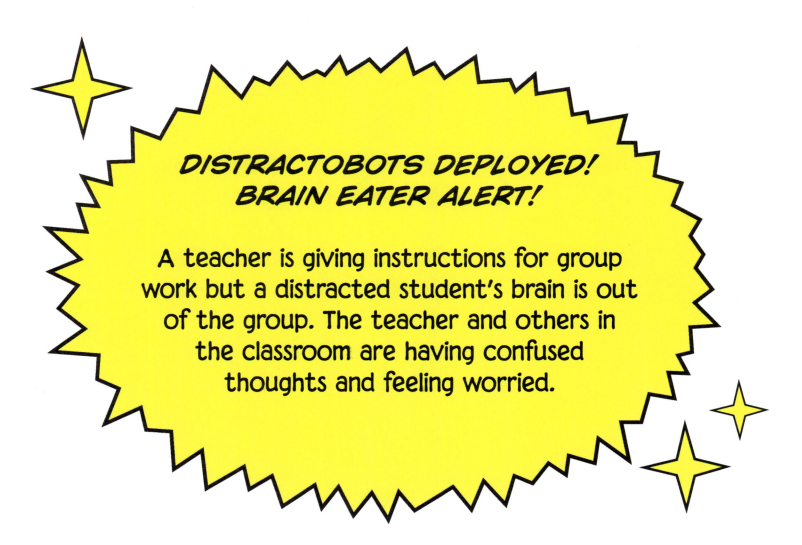

DISTRACTOBOTS DEPLOYED! BRAIN EATER ALERT!

A teacher is giving instructions for group work but a distracted student's brain is out of the group. The teacher and others in the classroom are having confused thoughts and feeling worried.

Superflex Aiden and Superflex Bark hurry to the classroom and can see the girl, Sarah, who is having a Brain Eater moment.

Superflex Aiden and Superflex Bark suddenly appear in the classroom. They remind Sarah to use her Focus Tron powers!

UNTHINKABOT & THINKABLE
Character Pairings

Our inner Superflex can work as a team with one or more Thinkables to provide good ideas and strategies to help manage the UnthinkaBots and their Bots. Below are some common UnthinkaBots you may find around Social Town and their paired Thinkables character counterparts.

UNTHINKABOTS ▼	▼ THINKABLES

Blurt Out Blue
I release **BlurtBots** to make people's thoughts pop out of their mouths when it's not their time to talk. BlurtBots also make people forget to use their eyes and brain to figure out if it's their turn to share.

Thought Catcher
I activate your **Thought Net** powers to help you figure out when it's a good time to keep thoughts in your brain and when it's time to say them aloud. I also help you to catch thoughts, write them down, file them in your thought keeper, or share them aloud.

Body Drifter
I send **DriftBots** to push and pull bodies away from others or make them wander away from where they are supposed to be.

Stick-Withem
I activate your **Sticky Senses** powers to help you to know when to stick with the group, stay near an adult, or stick with others.

UNTHINKABOT & THINKABLE
Character Pairings

UNTHINKABOTS ▼	▼ THINKABLES

Brain Eater
I stick **DistractoBots** into brains to make things like technology, games, and other thoughts distract from our focus on people and what is happening.

Focus Tron
I activate your **Focus Pocus** powers to pick and use your best strategy (fidget, break, move, shield, etc.) for keeping your brain connected to what is happening around you.

D.O.F. (Destroyer of Fun)
I throw **CompetiBots** at people during games or activities to make them overly competitive!

I.O.F. (Inventor of Fun)
I activate your **Cranium Coach** powers to coach your brain into positive self-talk and deep breathing during competitive times.

Energy Hare-y
I spring **EnergyBots** into people's bodies to make them use more or less energy than needed for what is happening and forget to use their energy managing strategies.

Aware Hare
I activate your **Energy Earbud** powers to help you figure out the level of energy needed for each activity.

Glassman
I send out **ExplodaBots** to make people get really upset and have gigantic responses, even when they have small problems.

Kool Q. Cumber
I activate your **Cooling Cap** powers to help your brain and body relax and your **Prob-u-lator** to figure out how big or small a problem feels.

UNTHINKABOT & THINKABLE
Character Pairings

UNTHINKABOTS ▼			▼ THINKABLES
Mean Bean — I toss **MeanBots** into brains to make people say or do mean things and to forget to think about others' feelings.			**Nice Light** — I activate your **Kind Mind** powers to remind you it's okay if people do things differently, look different, or play with different things, and to use self-talk to keep mean thoughts in your brain and avoid mean actions.
Me-Gull — I send flying **MeBots** into brains to make people focus on their Me-plans and only think about what they want to do and say.			**We-Gulls** — We activate **P.O.W.** or the **Power of We** to help you use people files, figure out the We-plan, and flex to others' ideas.
Rock Brain — I deploy **StuckBots** to get people really stuck on doing things one way, focusing only on their ideas, or forgetting to ask for help.			**T-Flex** — I activate your **Flex-a-Do** powers to flex what you do and say and try things another way.
Space Invader — I send **CloseBot** flares to make people pop into other people's space bubble or touch others' stuff by crossing their stuff bubble.			**Space Base** — I activate your **Space Base Radar** to help you measure the place to figure out the space in your own and others' personal space bubble.

UNTHINKABOT & THINKABLE
Character Pairings

UNTHINKABOTS ▼		▼ THINKABLES
Topic Twistermeister — I fling **TwistaBots** to make people say unrelated comments during *topic time* or forget to connect their thoughts to others during *talking time*.		**Tracker** — I activate your **Situation Sniffer** powers to help you sniff out the clues to figure out if it's *topic time* or just a *talking time*.
Un-Wonderer — I send out **UnwonderBots** to make people forget to ask wonder questions or socially wonder about others.	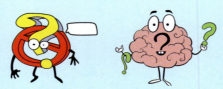	**The Wonderer** — I activate your **Wonder-full Wondering** powers to help you notice others and ask them wonder questions to store in your people files.
WasFunnyOnce — I sling **SillyBots** all around to make people miss cues for when it's a serious time or a silly time or when it's best to silence the sillies.		**Dr. HumorUs** — I activate your **Funny Finder** powers to help you figure out if the place, the people, and the time are a good fit for funniness.
Worry Wall — I stack and magnify **WorryBots** in people's brains to make them think they need to be perfect and avoid people and things.		**Worry WiseWorm** — I activate your **Worry Wisdom** to help you use clues to figure out if your worry is a Wee-Tiny Worry, a Wise Worry, or a WorryBot.

Superflex Quiz Answers

There are many correct responses and possible answers to the quizzes you've taken throughout the book, so don't worry if your answers do not match the ones below.

Superflex Quiz #1:
Can you think of three morning TO DO lists that you do at home to help yourself get ready for school?

Possible answers: make my lunch, brush my teeth, make my bed

Superflex Quiz #2:
Where would you put your Superflex Distracter Shield at home? At school?

Possible answers: on my computer, over my phone, on my gaming system

Superflex Quiz #3:
How do you feel when you quickly finish your TO DOs at home? At school?

Possible answers: relieved, happy, okay, thrilled, calm, excited

Superflex Quiz #4:
How did you do today getting your chores done at home?

Possible answer: I got distracted playing with my dog and my mom had to remind me so she was probably feeling frustrated. I quickly managed Brain Eater though and finished my chores.

Superflex Quiz #5:
Can you think of one Inside the Brain Distracter (ITBD) and one Outside the Brain Distracter (OTBD) that take your brain off track?

ITBD: Brain gets stuck thinking about my favorite Superflex cartoons.

OTBD: My Superflex storybook collection.

Superflex Quiz #6:
Give an example of your brain rolling away from the group and your body rolling away from the group.

Brain rolling away example: I was eating breakfast with mom and she was talking about the weekend, but my brain was thinking about the comic book I was reading and how it was going to end. I think that was very confusing for my mom because when she asked me a question, I could not answer it because I wasn't paying attention.

Body rolling away from the group: I was in class working in a group and I wanted to see the new computer in class so I got up and walked over to it. I wasn't thinking about how this would make my group mates feel. They were also probably worried or confused that I was leaving their group and wasn't going to help.

The Superflex® Series
Curriculum, storybooks, visual supports, tools, and games

Books

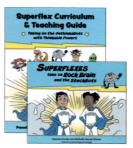

Posters

Music

Games

Stickers

Read hundreds of free articles on our website, including:
• Superflex® Teaches Super Metacognitive Strategies
• 10 DOs and DON'Ts for Teaching Superflex

Check out our On Demand Series on Superflex:
•Social Detective, Superflex®, and Friends Take on Social Emotional Learning

To learn more, visit www.socialthinking.com

SocialThinking has so much to offer!

OUR MISSION

At Social Thinking, our mission is to help people develop social competencies to better connect with others and experience deeper well-being. We create unique teaching frameworks and strategies to help individuals develop their social thinking and social emotional learning to meet their academic, personal, and professional social goals. These goals often include sharing space effectively with others, learning to work as part of a team, and developing relationships of all kinds: with family, friends, classmates, co-workers, romantic partners, etc.

FREE ARTICLES & WEBINARS

100+ free educational articles and webinars about our teaching strategies

LIVESTREAM EVENTS, ON DEMAND COURSES & CUSTOM TRAINING

Live and recorded trainings for schools and organizations

PRODUCTS

Print and ebooks, games, decks, posters, music and more!

CLINICAL RESEARCH

Measuring the effectiveness of the Social Thinking® Methodology

SERVICES: CHILDREN & ADULTS

Clinical services, assessments, school consultations, etc.

CLINICAL TRAINING PROGRAM

Three-day intensive training for professionals

www.socialthinking.com